Lop Rabbits

The Complete Lop Rabbit Pet Care Guide

Lop Rabbit Breeding, Buying, Care, Cost, Keeping, Health, Supplies, Food, Rescue and More Included!

By Lolly Brown

Foreword

Lop rabbits make wonderful pets with their soft, silky coats and long, floppy ears. They are also a great choice if you want a pet that will enjoy spending time with you! It is important to realize, however, that there are many different types of lop rabbits and each breed is special in its own unique way. Before you commit to becoming a rabbit owner, take the time to learn as much as you can about lop rabbits – this will help you decide whether a lop rabbit is right for you and, if it is, which breed is the best fit!

If you think that the lop rabbit might be the right pet for you, take the time to learn as much about these wonderful creatures as you can. In this book you will find a wealth of information about these beautiful animals including general facts about different breeds as well as practical information for keeping lop rabbits. By the time you finish this book you will have a thorough understanding of lop rabbits and you will know for sure whether or not they are the right pet for you.

So, if you are ready to learn more about lop rabbits just turn the page and keep reading!

Table of Contents

Introduction 1

    Glossary of Rabbit Terms 3

Chapter One: Understanding Lop Rabbits 2

    What are Lop Rabbits? 3

    Types of Lop Rabbits 6

    Lop Rabbit Colors and Patterns 12

Chapter Two: Things to Know Before Getting a Lop Rabbit
.... 16

    Do You Need a License? 17

    How Many Lop Rabbits Should You Keep? 19

    Do Lop Rabbits Get Along with Other Pets? 20

    How Much Does it Cost to Keep a Lop Rabbit? ... 21

        Initial Costs 22

        Monthly Costs 25

    What are the Pros and Cons of Lop Rabbits? 28

Chapter Three: Purchasing Your Lop Rabbit 30

    Where Can You Buy Lop Rabbits? 31

    How to Choose a Reputable Rabbit Breeder 34

    Tips for Selecting a Healthy Lop Rabbit 36

Chapter Four: Caring for Your Lop Rabbit 40

    Habitat Requirements for Lop Rabbits 41

a.) Choosing a Rabbit Cage 42

b.) Indoor Cages vs. Outdoor Hutches 43

c.) Recommended Cage Accessories 44

Litter Training Your Rabbit 45

Handling and Taming Your Rabbit 47

Chapter Five: Meeting Your Rabbit's Nutritional Needs 50

The Nutritional Needs of Rabbits 51

Tips for Feeding Lop Rabbits 54

Dangerous Foods to Avoid 56

Chapter Six: Breeding Your Lop Rabbit 58

Basic Rabbit Breeding Information 59

Raising Baby Lop Rabbits 61

Chapter Seven: Grooming Your Lop Rabbit 64

Recommended Tools to Have on Hand 65

Tips for Bathing and Grooming Lop Rabbits 67

Other Grooming Tasks 68

Chapter Eight: Showing Lop Rabbits 72

Lop Rabbit Breed Standards 73

Preparing Your Rabbit for Show 82

Chapter Nine: Keeping Your Rabbit Healthy 86

Common Health Problems Affecting Rabbits 87

Preventing Illness 97

Rabbit Care Sheet 100

    1.) Habitat Requirements..................................... 101

    2.) Nutritional Needs 102

    3.) Breeding Information 103

References... 106

Index... 110

Introduction

The term "lop rabbit" refers not to a specific breed of rabbit but to a certain type. The word "lop" is used to describe a rabbit whose ears hang down on either side of his head instead of standing up straight. Lop rabbits, or lop-eared rabbits, are cute and cuddly but they are not necessarily the right pet for everyone. Like any pet, lop rabbits require a lot of time and care in order to keep them happy and healthy. You shouldn't get a lop rabbit unless you are fully prepared for the responsibility.

Within the pages of this book you will receive a wealth of knowledge and fun facts about lop rabbits to help you understand more about these beautiful creatures. There are many different types of lop rabbits, but all of them make wonderful pets if you have the time to dedicate to their care. In reading this book you will learn everything you need to know to decide whether or not a lop rabbit is right for you and, if it is, you will be well on your way to becoming the best rabbit owner you can be!

So, if you are ready to learn more about the lop rabbit, simply turn the page and keep reading!

Glossary of Rabbit Terms

Agouti – A type of coloring in which the hair shaft has three or more bands of color with a definite break between.

Albino – A pink-eyed, white-furred rabbit.

ARBA – The American Rabbit Breeders Association; an organization which promotes rabbits in the United States.

Awn – The strong, straight guard hairs protruding above the undercoat in angora breeds.

Balance – An orderly and pleasing arrangement of physical characteristics promoting a harmonious appearance.

Bangs – Longer fur appearing at the front base of the ears and on top of the head in some woolen breeds.

Base Color – The color of the fur next to the skin.

Bell Ears – Ears that have large tips with distinct lop or fall.

Belt – The line where the colored portion of the coat meets the white portion, just behind the shoulders.

Blaze – A white marking found on the head of the Dutch rabbit; the shape is wedge-like.

Bonding – A term used to describe two rabbits that have paired up together.

BRC – The British Rabbit Council, formed from the British Rabbit Society and the National Rabbit Council of Great Britain in 1934.

Broken Coat – A coat with guard hairs missing or broken in places, exposing the undercoat

Buck – An unaltered or intact male rabbit.

Buff – A rich, golden-orange color.

Caecotroph – Pellets of semi-digested food eaten from the anus for nutrition reasons.

Chinning – Rubbing the chin on objects of people to spread scent from glands under the chin.

Cobby – A term meaning stout or stocky in body; short legs.

Condition – The overall physical state of a rabbit in terms of its fur, health, cleanliness, and grooming.

Crossbreeding – Mating two different breeds.

Cull – The process of selecting the best rabbits from a litter and selling or slaughtering the rest.

Dam – A female rabbit that has produced offspring.

Doe – An unaltered female rabbit.

Flat Coat – Fur lying too close to the body, lacking spring and body as noted by touch.

Flopping – A sign of happiness or contentedness; the rabbit flops over on his side and exposes his belly.

Fryer – A young meat rabbit no more than 10 weeks of age and weighing less than 5 pounds.

Gestation – The period of time between breeding and birthing (or kindling).

Guard Hair – The long, coarser hairs in a rabbit's coat which protect the undercoat.

Herd – A group of rabbits.

Inbreeding – Breeding of closely related stock.

Junior – A class of rabbits referring to those under 6 months of age.

Kindling – The process of giving birth to baby rabbits (kits).

Kindling Box – A box provided for a pregnant rabbit so she can make a nest and give birth.

Kit – A baby rabbit.

Line Breeding – A breeding program in which rabbits that are descended from the same animal are bred.

Litter – A group of young rabbits born to one doe at the same time.

Loose Coat – A condition of fur lacking density in the undercoat, often coupled with fine guard hairs resulting in a lack of texture.

Malocclusion – A misalignment of the rabbit's teeth.

Molt – The process of shedding or changing the fur, happens twice each year.

Nest Box – A box provided for a pregnant rabbit so she can make a nest and give birth.

Nursing – The process of kits suckling milk from the dam's teats; usually occurs twice a day.

Peanut – A rabbit with two dwarf genes; usually fatal.

Pelage – The fur coat or covering in a rabbit.

Pellets – May refer either to the rabbit's poop or its food.

Quick – The pink part of the nails/claws that contains the blood vessels and nerves.

Racy – Referring to a slim, slender body and legs.

Saddle – The rounded portion of the back between the rabbit's shoulder and loin.

Self-Colored – A fur pattern where the hair colors are the same all over the body.

Sire – A male rabbit that has produced offspring.

Thumping – The practice of banging or stomping the hind legs on the ground to make a loud, thudding noise.

Ticking - A wavy distribution of longer guard hairs throughout the rabbit's coat.

Weaning – The process in which baby rabbits become independent of their dam, transitioning to solid food.

Wool – A term used to describe the fur of Angora rabbits.

Chapter One: Understanding Lop Rabbits

You don't have to be a dog owner to understand that there are many different breeds of dog. What you may not know, however, is that the same applies to rabbits! The American Rabbit Breeders' Association (ARBA) currently recognizes about 48 unique breeds of rabbit, though the British Rabbit Council (BRC) currently recognizes more than 60 breeds. Of all the rabbit breeds in the world today (including those not yet recognized by the ARBA or the BRC), there are 19 different lop rabbit breeds.

What you need to know about lop rabbits is that they are not a specific breed. Rather, the word "lop" simply describes a particular type of ear in rabbits – ears that hang down on either side of the head instead of standing straight up. So, all of those 19 breeds may be very different in terms of size, coat, and color but they have one thing in common – lop ears. In this chapter you will learn the basics about lop-eared rabbits and you will be introduced to some of the most popular lop rabbit breeds.

What are Lop Rabbits?

As you have already learned, lop rabbits are simply rabbits that have ears which hang down on either side of their head (see the picture at the beginning of this chapter). Though there are 19 different breeds of lop rabbits in the world, only 5 of them are actually recognized by the ARBA in the United States and the BRC recognizes 9 different lop breeds. Below you will find a list of the lop breeds recognized by the ARBA and the BRC.

Lop Breeds Recognized by the ARBA:

- American Fuzzy Lop
- English Lop
- French Lop
- Holland Lop
- Miniature Lop

Lop Breeds Recognized by the BRC:

- Cashmere Lop
- Cashmere Miniature Lop
- Dwarf Lop
- English Lop
- French Lop
- German Lop
- Meissner Lop
- Miniature Lop
- Miniature Lion Lop

When it comes to differentiating between different breeds of rabbits, there are more factors to consider than ear type. Another major distinguishing factor between different types of rabbits is fur type. Some rabbits (like Rex breeds) have very short, velvety fur while others have long fur (like the American Fuzzy Lop and the Angora rabbit). There are also rabbits with medium fur.

In addition to considering the rabbit's fur, you must also take the rabbit's body shape into consideration. The ARBA identifies five different body shapes in rabbits:

- **Full Arch** – A rabbit with an arched back starting at the nape of the neck, arching to the tail.
- **Semi-Arch (or Mandolin)** – A rabbit with an arched back that starts behind the shoulders and arches to the tail.
- **Compact** – These rabbits are lighter and shorter in length than meat rabbits, usually kept for show or kept as pets.
- **Cylindrical** – A rabbit having a long, thin, rounded body with small bones and a long, slender head.
- **Commercial** – Rabbits that are medium in size with bodies about as wide as they are deep.

Another way to categorize the different rabbit breeds is by purpose. There are three general types for rabbits –

meat, fur, and wool. Meat rabbits include the larger breeds like the Californian and New Zealand breeds – they grow quickly and are usually ready for slaughter by about 8 to 12 weeks of age. Fur rabbits are bred for their soft, thick fur which can be used for coats and trim on clothing. Examples of fur rabbits include Rex and Mini Rex – some fur rabbits are also meat rabbits. The third type is the wool type – these are rabbits which produce wool in the same way that a sheep produces wool. Examples of wool rabbits include Jersey Woolies and Angora rabbits.

Types of Lop Rabbits

Now that you understand what differentiates the different rabbit breeds you are ready to learn a little bit more about the different lop breeds. In this section you will find a brief overview of the lop rabbit breeds that are accepted by the ARBA and the BRC.

American Fuzzy Lop (ARBA)

The American Fuzzy Lop has a short, close-coupled body and weighs no more than 4 pounds at maturity. This breed has a dense, wooly coat that is slightly course in nature. The length should be at least 2 inches and should be uniform all over the body. This breed is heavily muscled, compact, and balanced with full, wide ears that lop vertically from the base and are well placed on top of the head. Recognized color groups include agouti, broken, pointed white, self, shaded, and white band.

Cashmere Lop (BRC)

The Cashmere Lop has a thickset, firm body that is short and well-muscled. The maximum weigh is 5 ¼ pounds, though the ideal weight is closer to 4 ½ pounds. These rabbits have dense fur measuring 1 ½ to 2 inches in length with the topcoat being longer and heavier than the undercoat. The ears are broad and thick with rounded tips, hanging close to the cheeks. The permitted color categories for this breed include self, agouti, shaded, and tan. There is also a

Miniature Cashmere Lop breed which weighs no more than 3 ½ pounds at maturity.

Dwarf Lop (BRC)

The Dwarf Lop is sometimes identified as the same breed as the Mini Lop, though there are actually some differences between the two. The Dwarf Lop is slightly larger, weighing up to 5 ¼ pounds at maturity with a minimum weight of 4 ¼ pounds. Dwarf Lops have short bodies with deep chests, wide shoulders, and short legs. These rabbits have a dense coat with broad, thick ears that are carried close to the cheeks. The accepted color categories for this breed include self, agouti, shaded, and tan.

English Lop (ARBA, BRC)

The English Lop is a large breed with a full, round chest and a mandolin shape. The average specimen of this breed weighs 11 to 12 pounds at maturity. This breed has long ears measuring at least 21 inches from tip to tip with proportionate width. The ears are soft and pliable, free from blemishes. The English Lop has medium-length fur that is fine and silky to the touch. It comes in the following color group – agouti, broken self, shaded, ticked, and wide band with or without colored markings.

French Lop (ARBA, BRC)

The French Lop has a massive, thick-set body with broad shoulders and a gently curving topline. This breed is the largest of the lop breeds, weighing 10 to 13 pounds at maturity. French Lops have glossy fur that averages 1 ¼ inches in length with uniform thickness and density. These rabbits can be shown in the following patterns: agouti, broken self, shaded, ticked, and wide band.

German Lop (BRC)

The German Lop is a medium-sized breed with a cobby body. These rabbits have a Roman nose with wide-set eyes and well-developed cheeks. The ears measure 11 to 14 inches long and they are broad and thick in substance, carried close to the cheeks. The coat is normal length and very dense with strong guard hairs. This rabbit breed comes in all recognized colors except the broken pattern. These rabbits weigh at least 8 ½ pounds at maturity.

Holland Lop (ARBA)

The Holland Lop has a short, thick set body with a broad chest and strong muscles. The ears hang close to the cheeks from a proper position on the crown – they are thick, wide, and well-rounded at the tips. This is the smallest of the lop breeds with adult show rabbits weighing between 2 and 4 pounds. The accepted color groups include agouti, broken, pointed white, self-shaded, tan pattern, ticked, and wide band. Rabbits are shown in two classifications – solid pattern and broken pattern.

Meissner Lop (BRC)

The Meissner Lop is medium-sized, weighing 7 ¾ to 10 pounds at maturity. This breed is a little less stocky than larger lop breeds with a broad chest and nicely arched back. The fur is medium-length and dense, interspersed with guard hairs. The ears measure 15 to 16 inches in length and they are set well on both sides. The Meissner Lop comes in the following accepted colors – black, blue, yellow, and Havana. The top color should be evenly silvered.

Mini Lop (ARBA, BRC)

Also sometimes called the Dwarf Lop, the Mini Lop is a fairly small breed but not the smallest breed in existence. These rabbits typically weigh between 5 ½ and 6 ½ pounds at maturity with a heavily muscled, compact and balanced body type. The Mini Lop has a medium-length coat that is glossy and lustrous as well as being thick and dense. The ears are well placed on the top of the head, hanging close to the cheeks. These rabbits can be shown in the following categories: agouti, broken, pointed white, self-shaded, ticked, and wide band. There are many accepted colors.

Mini Lion Lop (BRC)

The Mini Lion Lop has a short, well-muscled body that is thickset and firm. It is a very small breed, weighing no more than 3.8 pounds with an ideal weight closer to 3.4 pounds. Mini Lion Lops have dense coats with a mane of longer fur around the neck measuring 2 to 3 inches in length – it also extends to a "V" along the back of the neck, running down the length of the rabbit to the tail. The ears are broad, thick, and well-furred with rounded tips. This breed comes in all colors and patterns accepted by the BRC except for the broken pattern.

Lop Rabbit Colors and Patterns

Different breeds of lop rabbits come in different colors and patterns. For the most detailed description of these colors and patterns, refer to the breed standards set forth by the ARBA and the BRC. If you want to get a general idea of lop rabbit colors and patterns, however, review the list provided below:

Agouti Pattern – The agouti pattern has a hair shaft that has three or more bands of color with a definite break in between each color. This pattern is usually dark slate at the base with two or more alternating bands of light or dark color. The head, feet, and ears are usually ticked and eye circles, belly, under the jaws, and underside of the tail are usually lighter in color with no ticking.

<u>Agouti Colorations Include</u>: chinchilla, chestnut, lynx, opal.

Broken Pattern – The broken pattern includes any recognized breed color in combination with white and carrying the breed pattern. The body pattern can be spotted, patches, or blanket with head markings to show color on both ears, on the nose, and both eye circles.

Self-Colored – The self-colored pattern consists of a single color all over the body, head, ears, feet, legs, and tail.

<u>Self-Colored Colorations Include</u>: black, blue, chocolate, lilac, and white

Shaded – The shaded pattern shows a gradual transition of a basic color, typically from dark to light. The darker color appears on the back, head, ears, tail, feet and leg areas, shading down to a lighter color on the belly and sides.

<u>Shaded Colorations Include</u>: frosted pearl, sable, sable point, seal, smoke pearl, and tortoise

Pointed White – The pointed white pattern consists of a body color of pure white with markings on the nose, ears, feet, and tail. Markings may be black, blue, chocolate, or lilac. The eye color is pink.

Ticked – The ticked pattern shows guard hairs interspersed throughout the coat, either solid or tipped, with a color distinct from the under-color or the surface color.

Ticked Colorations Include: silver, silver fox, and steel

Wide Band – The wide band pattern consists of the same coloration over the body, head, ears, tail, and feet. May include a lighter coloration on the eye circles, inside the ears, under the tail, jowls, and belly areas.

White Band Colorations Include: cream, fawn, orange, red.

Chapter Two: Things to Know Before Getting a Lop Rabbit

Now that you know a little about what a lop rabbit is and what breeds exist, you may be thinking that it is the ideal pet for you. Before you actually go out and buy a lop rabbit, however, you need to consider some of the more practical aspects of rabbit care and ownership. In this chapter you will learn the basics about licensing requirements for pet rabbits as well as the associated costs of ownership. You will also receive helpful information about keeping your rabbit with other pets and for keeping more than one rabbit at a time.

Do You Need a License?

Before you bring home a new pet, it is always a good idea to determine whether there are any laws in your area which require you to register or license your pet. In many cases, a license or permit is only required for exotic or endangered animals – lop rabbits do not qualify. There are, however, some local regulations which may require you to license your rabbit. For example, the state of Minnesota requires rabbit owners to license their pets at $15 a year – the cost may be higher if the rabbit is not spayed or neutered.

If you plan to breed and sell rabbits, you may be subject to an entirely different set of regulations. According to the Animal and Plant Health Inspection Service (APHIS)

Animal Welfare Act, your business must be licensed unless you are only selling rabbits for meat or fiber. If you sell rabbits as pets, you do not need a license if your annual sales are under $500. As always, however, it is a good idea to research the regulations in your area before you do anything – it is better to be safe than sorry.

Licensing regulations in the U.K. are always a bit different from the United States. For example, rabbit owners are not required to obtain a license or permit for their rabbits. If you plan to import a rabbit from outside the U.K. or export one outside the country, however, you will need to obtain an animal movement license (AML). This rule is in place because rabies has been eradicated from the U.K. and unregulated imports and exports of live animals could re-introduce the disease.

How Many Lop Rabbits Should You Keep?

For the most part, rabbits are naturally very social creatures so they enjoy being kept with other rabbits. It is not necessarily a requirement that you keep two of the same kind of rabbit either – as long as they are similar in size and their cage provides ample space for both, you can keep different breeds of lop rabbits together. The best way to ensure harmony among your rabbits is to raise them together from a young age – ideally younger than 12 weeks. If you keep more than two rabbits together, make sure there is no more than one male for every two females. The best combination is an altered male and female pair or a pair of brothers or sisters.

Do Lop Rabbits Get Along with Other Pet.

There is no simple "Yes" or "No" answer to this question because there are many factors to consider. For one thing, the individual temperament of lop rabbits vary from one rabbit to another – some rabbits might be very docile and unflappable while others may be a little more nervous and high-strung. You also have to consider the temperament of your dog or cat. Some dogs have a very low prey drive so you don't really have to worry about them chasing your rabbit around. Other breeds, however, particularly terriers and other hunting breeds, have a very high prey drive and if your rabbit has a high flight response, it could lead to a dangerous chase.

When it comes to lop rabbits getting along with cats, the response is also highly varied. Smaller breeds of lop rabbit like the Mini Lion Lop or the Dwarf Lop may look more like prey to a cat than a larger rabbit like the English Lop. If your rabbit is larger than your cat, it probably won't be a problem but you still need to be careful. The best thing to do is to introduce your pets to each other while they are still young so they grow up together. Even then, you should still supervise their interactions to be safe.

How Much Does it Cost to Keep a Lop Rabbit?

Many inexperienced rabbit owners make the mistake of thinking that a rabbit is a cheap pet. While it may not cost you much to purchase a rabbit, there are many other expenses you need to consider. You need to house your rabbit, provide him with a healthy diet, and make sure that he gets regular veterinary care. The costs associated with rabbit ownership can be divided into two categories: initial costs and monthly costs. You will receive an overview of these costs as well as an estimate for each in the following pages of this section.

Initial Costs

The initial costs for keeping a lop rabbit include those costs that you must cover before you can bring your rabbit home. Some of the initial costs you will need to cover include your rabbit's cage, food/water equipment, toys and accessories, initial vaccinations, spay/neuter surgery and supplies for grooming and nail clipping – it also includes the cost of the rabbit itself. <u>You will find an overview of each of these costs as well as an estimate for each below</u>:

Purchase Price – The cost to purchase a lop rabbit can vary greatly depending on the breed and where you buy him. You can probably find a backyard breeder offering $10 (£9) rabbits, but you cannot be sure of the breeding quality for these rabbits. Generally speaking, pet-quality rabbits sell for $15 to $50 (£13.50 to £45), depending on the breed. If you want to invest in a show-quality rabbit, you may have to pay a little more – upwards of $50 (£45) and as much as $250 (£225) for some breeds.

Cage or Hutch – Rabbits are fairly active animals so they need a cage or hutch large enough that they have space to move around. It is also a good idea to let your rabbit out of the cage on a daily basis, but the cage still needs to be fairly large. Depending on the size of the cage and the materials from which it is made, you can expect to spend between $50 and $150 (£45 to £135).

Food/Water Bowls – In addition to providing your lop rabbit with a cage or hutch, you should also make sure he has a set of high-quality food bowls and a water bottle. The best materials food bowls is stainless steel because it is easy to clean and doesn't harbor bacteria – ceramic is another good option. The average cost for a quality stainless steel bowl and a rabbit water bottle is about $20 (£18).

Toys – Toys for rabbits fill two purposes. For one thing, they help to provide the rabbit with mental and physical stimulation to prevent boredom. Many toys can also be used as chew toys to help wear down your rabbit's teeth. You might want to start off with an assortment of different toys to see which kind your rabbit likes. Plan to budget a cost of $50 (£45) for toys just to be sure you have enough.

Initial Vaccinations – Rabbits don't need as many vaccinations as cats and dogs, but they should be vaccinated for calcivirus around 12 weeks of age. Your veterinarian can tell you if your rabbit needs any other vaccinations. To cover the cost of these vaccinations you should budget about $20 (£18) just to be prepared.

Spay/Neuter Surgery – If you don't plan to breed your lop rabbit you should seriously consider having have him or her neutered or spayed. Unfortunately, the cost to spay or neuter a small mammal is fairly high – around $50 to $150 (£45 to £135). If you keep two rabbits of the same sex together, it may not be necessary.

Supplies/Accessories – In addition to purchasing your rabbit's cage and other accessories, you should also purchase some basic grooming supplies like nail clippers, a brush, and mild antiseptic ear-cleaning solution. You should also purchase a litter box if you want to litter train your rabbit.

The cost for these items will vary depending on the quality, but you should budget about $50 (£45) for these extra costs.

Initial Costs for Lop Rabbits		
Cost	**One Rabbit**	**Two Rabbits**
Purchase Price	$10 - $250 (£9 - £225)	$20 - $500 (£18 - £450)
Cage or Hutch	$50 to $150 (£45 to £135)	$50 to $150 (£45 to £135)
Food/Water Equipment	$20 (£18)	$40 (£36)
Toys	$50 (£45)	$100 (£90)
Vaccinations	$20 (£18)	$40 (£32)
Spay/Neuter	$50 to $150 (£45 to £135)	$100 to $300 (£90 - £270)
Accessories	$50 (£45)	$50 (£45)
Total	$250 to $690 (£225 – £621)	$400 to $1,180 (£360 – £1,062)

*Costs may vary depending on location
**U.K. prices based on an estimated exchange of $1 = £0.90

Monthly Costs

The monthly costs for keeping a lop rabbit as a pet include those costs which recur on a monthly basis. The most important monthly cost for keeping a rabbit is, of course, food. In addition to food, however, you'll also need to think about things like your bedding, litter, toy replacements, and veterinary exams. <u>You will find an overview of each of these costs as well as an estimate for each cost in the following pages</u>:

Food and Treats – Feeding your lop rabbit a healthy diet is very important for his health and wellness. Rabbits usually eat about 1 ounce of food per pound of bodyweight, so you can expect a 5-pound rabbit to eat about 9 pounds of food per month. Rabbit pellets usually run about $8 or so for 5 pounds of food. For a lop rabbit, you should budget about $10 to $20 (£9 to £18) per month for food, depending on the rabbit's breed and size. You should also provide your rabbit with fresh hay and vegetables which can run an extra $10 (£9) a month or so.

Bedding and Litter – Whether or not you need bedding for your rabbit cage will depend on the type of cage you use. Even if you don't use bedding in the whole cage, you should still provide some kind of hideaway lined with comfy bedding for your lop rabbit to sleep in. You will also need to replace your rabbit's litter once in a while. You should plan to spend about $20 (£18) a month on bedding and litter for your rabbit cage.

Veterinary Exams – In order to keep your rabbit healthy you should take him to the veterinarian about every six months or so. The average cost for a vet visit for a rabbit is about $40 (£26) so, if you have two visits per year, it averages to about $7 (£4.55) per month.

Other Costs – In addition to the monthly costs for your rabbit's food, bedding, litter, and vet visits there are also some other cost you might have to pay occasionally. These costs might include things like replacements for worn-out toys as well as cleaning products. You should budget about $15 (£9.75) per month for extra costs.

Monthly Costs for Sphynx Cats		
Cost	**One Cat**	**Two Cats**
Food and Treats	$20 to $30 (£18 to £27)	$40 to $60 (£32 to £54)
Bedding/Litter	$20 (£18)	$20 (£18)
Veterinary Exams	$7 (£4.55)	$14 (£12.60)

Other Costs	$15 (£9.75)	$30 (£19.50)
Total	$62 to $72	$104 to $124
	(£56 to £65)	(£94 to £112)

*Costs may vary depending on location
**U.K. prices based on an estimated exchange of $1 = £0.90

What are the Pros and Cons of Lop Rabbits?

Before choosing a lop rabbit for a pet, you need to think about the upsides as well as the downsides. It is also important to remember that there are many different lop rabbit breeds and the specific pros and cons may vary slightly as such. <u>Below you will find a list of pros and cons for lop rabbits in general</u>:

Pros for the Lop Rabbit

- Lop rabbits come in a variety of sizes depending on the breed – allows you to choose the best option.
- Generally a good pet for smaller living spaces such as condos and apartments.
- Lop rabbits are easily trained to use a litter box - makes it easy to clean up after them.
- Generally a friendly, docile pet – can be a good choice for responsible children.
- Lop rabbits are easy to care for in terms of their diet – they eat mainly pellets, hay, and fresh veggies.

Cons for the Lop Rabbit

- Rabbits cannot be kept in their cages 24/7 – they need space and time to explore.
- May not be a good choice for a household that already has cats and/or dogs.
- Generally not recommended for very young children who don't know how to handle a rabbit.
- Some lop rabbits require a lot of grooming – particularly long-coated varieties.
- Can be a long-term commitment – most rabbits live anywhere from 8 to 12 years.

Chapter Three: Purchasing Your Lop Rabbit

Now that you have a better understanding of what it is like to keep a lop rabbit as a pet, you may be thinking that it is the right pet for you! If so, your next step is to figure out where you are going to get your lop rabbit and whether you want a baby rabbit or an adult. In this chapter you will receive some basic tips for finding a lop rabbit breeder and for choosing one that is reputable and trustworthy. You will also receive tips for picking out a baby rabbit that is healthy and well-bred.

Where Can You Buy Lop Rabbits?

Because there are so many lop rabbit breeds to choose from, you need to do some research and decide which breed you want before you start shopping around. When you are ready to buy a lop rabbit, you then need to start thinking about where you are going to get it. You may be able to find a lop rabbit at your local pet store, but think carefully before you buy whether that is really the best option. When you buy a rabbit from a pet store you have no way of knowing where the rabbit came from – you also don't know anything about the quality of its breeding.

If you want a baby rabbit, your best bet is to find a local lop rabbit breeder. Before you go down that road, however, consider whether adopting an adult rabbit might be the better option for you. There are plenty of adult rabbits out there who have been abandoned by their previous owners and they are looking for a new forever home. When you adopt a rabbit you are actually saving a life and there are some benefits for you as well! Adopting a rabbit can sometimes be cheaper than buying from a breeder and, in many cases, you get a cage and accessories with the adoption. Many adult rabbits ready for adoption have also already been spayed or neutered, litter trained, and they will be caught up on vaccinations.

If you are thinking about adopting a lop rabbit, consider one of these rescues:

United States Rescues:

Luv-a-Bun Rabbit Rescue. <http://bunnyrabbit.org/>

BunSpace Rabbit Rescue. <http://www.bunspace.com/>

Erie Area Rabbit Society and Rescue.
<http://www.eriearearabbitsociety.org/>

Long Island Rabbit Rescue Group.
<http://www.longislandrabbitrescue.org/happy_tails.htm>

Magic Happens Rabbit Rescue.
<http://www.magichappensrescue.com/>

The Bunny Bunch Rescue.
<http://www.bunnybunch.org/pages/>

United Kingdom Rescues:

Rabbit Rehome.
<http://www.rabbitrehome.org.uk/breeds.asp>

Southampton Rabbit Rescue.
http://www.southamptonrabbitrescue.org.uk/>

Cotton Tails Rescue. <http://www.cottontails-rescue.org.uk/>

The Cat & Rabbit Rescue Centre. <http://www.crrc.co.uk/>

Fairly Beloved Rabbit Care. < http://www.fbrc.org.uk/>

Acomb Rabbit Rescue.
<http://www.acombrabbitrescue.org.uk/>

How to Choose a Reputable Rabbit Breeder

To make sure that you get a well-bred, healthy lop rabbit of your chosen breed, your best bet is to look around for a local breeder. You can feel free to ask around at your local pet store and you may also be able to get a personal recommendation from friends or your local veterinarian. Once you Once you have your list of breeders on hand you can go through them one-by-one to narrow down your options. <u>Go through the following steps to weed out low-quality breeders and to choose the best option</u>:

- Visit the website for each breeder on your list (if they have one) and look for key information about the breeder's history and experience.

- o Check for ARBA or BRC registrations and a license, if applicable.
- o If the website doesn't provide any information about the facilities or the breeder you are best just moving on.
- After ruling out some of the breeders, contact the remaining breeders on your list by phone
  - o Ask the breeder questions about his experience with breeding rabbits in general and about the specific lop rabbit breed you are looking for.
  - o Ask for information about the breeding stock including registration numbers and health information.
  - o Expect a reputable breeder to ask you questions about yourself as well – a responsible breeder wants to make sure that his rabbits go to good homes.
- Schedule an appointment to visit the facilities for the remaining breeders on your list after you've weeded a few more of them out.
  - o Ask for a tour of the facilities, including the place where the breeding stock is kept as well as the facilities housing the baby rabbits.
  - o If things look unorganized or unclean, do not purchase from the breeder.

- o Make sure the breeding stock is in good condition and that the baby rabbits are all healthy-looking and active.
- Narrow down your list to a final few options and then interact with the rabbits to make your decision.
  - o Make sure the breeder provides some kind of health guarantee and ask about any vaccinations the rabbits may already have.
- Put down a deposit, if needed, to reserve a rabbit if they aren't ready to come home yet.

Tips for Selecting a Healthy Lop Rabbit

After you have narrowed down your list of options to just two or three lop rabbit breeders, your next step is to actually pick out the baby rabbit you want. You have already determined that the remaining breeders on your list are responsible, but now you need to make sure that the baby rabbits they have available are healthy and ready to go home with their new owners. <u>Follow the steps below to pick out your lop rabbit</u>:

- Ask the breeder to give you a tour of the facilities.
  - o Make sure the facilities where the rabbits are housed is clean and sanitary – if there is evidence of diarrhea, do not purchase one of the rabbits because they may already be sick.
- Take a few minutes to observe the litter as a whole, watching how the rabbits interact with each other.
  - o The baby rabbits should be active and playful, interacting with each other in a healthy way.
  - o Avoid any rabbits that appear to be lethargic and those that have difficulty moving – they could be sick.
- Put your hand into the cage or nesting box and give the baby rabbits time to sniff and explore you before you interact with them.
  - o Pet the baby rabbits and encourage them to play with a toy, taking the opportunity to observe their personalities.
  - o Single out any of the rabbits that you think might be a good fit and spend a little more time with them.

- Pick up the baby rabbit and hold him to see how he responds to human contact.
  - o The baby rabbit might squirm a little but it shouldn't be frightened of you and it should enjoy being pet.
- Examine the rabbit's body for signs of any illness and potential injury
  - o The baby rabbit should have clear, bright eyes with no discharge.
  - o The ears should be clean and clear with no discharge or inflammation.
  - o The baby rabbit stomach may be round but it shouldn't be distended or swollen.
  - o The baby rabbit should be able to walk and run normally without any mobility problems.
- Narrow down your options and choose the baby rabbit that you think is the best fit.

Chapter Four: Caring for Your Lop Rabbit

Now that you have picked out your rabbit, your next task is to get your home ready for him! Rabbits make wonderful pets and they are surprisingly easy to care for in many ways. Still, your lop rabbit has certain habitat requirements that you need to meet in order for him to remain happy and healthy. In this chapter you will learn the basics about your rabbit's habitat requirements including the recommended cage type, useful accessories, and exercise requirements. You will also receive tips for litter training and for taming and handling your lop rabbit.

Habitat Requirements for Lop Rabbits

One of the greatest things about keeping a lop rabbit as a pet is that you do not necessarily need a cage! As long as your rabbit is litter-trained, you can let him roam freely around the house if it is safe to do so. Even if you do let your rabbit out to roam around, however, it is never a bad idea to have a backup cage or, at least, somewhere the rabbit can hide and rest if he wants to. Keep reading to learn the basics about your rabbit's habitat requirements. You will also learn about recommended cage accessories and receive tips for choosing the right bedding for your rabbit.

a.) Choosing a Rabbit Cage

When it comes to choosing a cage for your rabbit there are several things to consider. The most important factor is, of course, the size of the cage. Rabbits are active animals so even if you let your rabbit out of the cage sometimes his cage should still be large enough that he can move around. At the least, your rabbit cage should be 4 to 6 times the length of your rabbit when he is fully stretched out. Because different lop rabbit breeds are different sizes, you'll have to do this measurement yourself.

Another factor you need to consider with your rabbit's cage is the materials from which it is made. You want to choose a cage that is easy to clean, so wooden cages are best avoided since they can absorb moisture and harbor bacteria. Generally speaking, plastic cages and metal cages are usually the best choice. Avoid cages with wire flooring, however, because these can irritate your rabbit's feet. If you have to choose a cage with a wire floor, cover a portion of it with a square of carpet or a mat – otherwise your rabbit will probably just hang out in his litter box.

If you don't want to let your rabbit run loose in the house, you should provide an exercise pen in addition to a large cage. The cage itself should provide at least 8 square feet of space for 1 to 2 rabbits and the exercise space should provide at least 24 square feet of space. Your rabbit should get at least 5 hours a day in the exercise pen or, if you are handy, you can connect the pen to his cage so he can come and go as he pleases.

b.) Indoor Cages vs. Outdoor Hutches

Many rabbit owners think that rabbits are best kept in outdoor hutches, but this may not necessarily be the case. There are, however, some important pros and cons to consider for outdoor rabbits. For example, it is easier to find space for a very large cage to house multiple rabbits outdoors – you also don't have to worry about noise or odors if you keep your rabbits outdoors. If you provide your rabbits with an outdoor run, they will be able to eat grass and other plants to supplement their diet without costing you any extra money. Plus, clean-up is easier for outdoor cages than for indoor cages.

On the other side of the issue, keeping rabbits outdoors may expose them to parasites and other dangerous diseases – especially if they come into contact with wild rabbits. If your rabbits are kept outdoors, they may not receive as much attention and human interaction as they might if they were kept inside. Keeping your rabbits outdoors puts them at risk for predation and they could also be exposed to extreme temperatures and inclement weather which could make them sick.

c.) Recommended Cage Accessories

In addition to providing your rabbit with a cage, you also need to stock it with certain accessories. Your rabbit doesn't need much but there are a few necessities such as a water bottle, food bowl, hay rack, litter pan, and a nest box or shelter. When it comes to your rabbit's water bottle, it is worth it to spend a few extra dollars for a non-drip model – this will keep you from having to change your bedding as frequently. You should also buy a hay rack to keep your rabbit's hay fresh by raising it up off the floor of the cage where it could be soiled.

Your rabbit's litter pan does not need to be anything fancy – it just needs to be large enough for your rabbit to turn around in and deep enough to contain the litter without making it hard for your rabbit to get into the pan. Other things your rabbit may need include chew toys and other toys to provide mental and physical stimulation. Buy an assortment of toys at first and give your rabbit time to play with them so you can learn which type of toys he prefers. Your rabbit also needs a hiding place or shelter.

Another thing you need to consider for your rabbit's cage is the type of litter you want to use – if you choose to use any at all. The best litter to use in a rabbit cage is fresh hay – ideally edible hay like meadow hay or timothy hay. You can also use a blanket made from some kind of natural fiber. Straw bedding and shredded newspaper or cardboard is not recommended for rabbit cages because it absorbs moisture which can lead to urine burn and it can also harbor bacteria. The worst bedding for rabbits is wood shavings, sawdust, cat litter, or any kind of cedar or pine product.

Litter Training Your Rabbit

Once you have set up your rabbit's cage, your next step is to litter train your rabbit. Rabbits are naturally fairly clean animals and they tend to choose one or two places in their cage to urinate and defecate. This makes your job very easy. All you have to do is watch your rabbit for a few days to determine where he tends to relieve himself and then simply place a litter pan in that area. Some rabbits choose a single location and others choose two or more – they are usually located in the corners of cage.

After discovering where your rabbit likes to relieve himself, you need to determine which type of litter you want to use. Avoid cat litters because they are often dusty or scented – you also don't want anything that clumps. The best litter to use is something organic made from alfalfa or oat hay, even paper. You can also simply use fresh hay as your litter! You want to avoid wood shavings, sawdust, and shredded newspaper or cardboard because they can absorb moisture. You also want to avoid anything made with cedar or pine because the natural oils can irritate your rabbit.

Handling and Taming Your Rabbit

Rabbits make wonderful pets for a number of reasons but one of those reasons is that they are easy to tame. The more time you spend with your rabbit, the more quickly he will get used to you and he will come to enjoy interacting with you. It is important to remember, however, that rabbits are fragile animals so you want to be careful about how you handle them. You must also remember that rabbits are prey animals so they dislike being picked up – if you do pick your rabbit up, hold him securely against your chest until you can sit down then place him on your lap.

If you are a new rabbit owner, it may take some practice to learn how to safely pick your rabbit up out of his cage. One thing you can do is use small treats to entice your rabbit to come to you. When he does, start gently petting him along the back until he seems calm enough for you to pick him up. When you do, make sure to support his body from underneath and then hold him securely against your chest to make sure he doesn't fall.

Chapter Five: Meeting Your Rabbit's Nutritional Needs

Although taking your lop rabbit to the vet once or twice a year is a good way to make sure he is in good health, there is something simple you can do that will have an even bigger impact on his health – feeding him a healthy diet. Rabbits require a certain balance of nutrients just like any other animal and it is your job to learn what your lop rabbit's needs are and to choose a pet food product that will meet them. In this chapter you'll learn about the nutritional needs of rabbits and receive some feeding tips.

The Nutritional Needs of Rabbits

Rabbits are herbivores which means that the entirety of their diet should be made up of plant products. It is also important to realize that rabbits have very high needs for fiber in their diet. Making sure that your rabbit's nutritional needs are met is actually quite simple – a balanced diet for rabbits should be made up of high-quality commercial pellets, fresh timothy hay, oat hay, and fresh vegetables. Your rabbit also needs constant access to fresh water because this too plays a role in your rabbit's digestion.

When choosing a high-quality commercial pellet to use as your rabbit's staple diet, there are a few things you should look for. First of all, the pellets should contain at least

18% fiber – the more the better. And make sure that the pellets you are buying are fresh. Do not purchase more than your rabbit can eat in 6 weeks' time because that is about as long as the pellets will remain fresh. After that point, they will lose some of their nutritional value and they won't provide your rabbit with the nutrients he needs.

In addition to choosing a quality pellet for your rabbit you should also stock up on fresh grass hay. Grass hay is loaded with calcium, vitamin A, vitamin D and other nutrients plus, the process of eating hay helps to keep your rabbit's digestive tract healthy and also helps to wear down his teeth. Your rabbit needs at least one type of grass hay – timothy hay is generally the easiest and most cost-effective option to find. He also needs some oat hay. Alfalfa hay is okay for young rabbits because it contains more protein than other hays but it should only be offered occasionally for adult rabbits because fiber is more important for them than protein. Like the pellets, you want to make sure that your hay stays fresh.

The final component of your rabbit's diet is fresh vegetables. You should aim to feed your rabbit about 1 cup of leafy greens per 2 pounds of bodyweight per day with a small amount of other vegetables – leafy greens are nutrient-dense and should comprise about 75% of your rabbit's fresh vegetable intake. Leafy greens include things like spinach, parsley, mustard greens, swiss chard, arugula, lettuce, dandelion greens, cilantro, and more. <u>Here is a list of non-leafy green vegetables that are also safe for rabbits</u>:

- Carrots
- Broccoli
- Edible flowers
- Celery
- Bell peppers
- Snow peas

- Brussel sprouts
- Cabbage (any type)
- Broccolini
- Summer squash
- Zucchini
- Wheat grass

In addition to fresh vegetables, you can also feed your rabbit small amounts of fresh fruit – these should comprise no more than 10% of your rabbit's fresh diet. Feed your rabbit no more than 1 teaspoon per 2 pounds of bodyweight on a daily basis. <u>Here are some fruits safe for lop rabbits</u>:

- Banana
- Melons
- Star Fruit
- Apricot
- Currants
- Nectarines
- Apple
- Cherries

- Pear
- Peach
- Plum
- Kiwi
- Papaya
- Mango
- Berries
- Pineapple

When feeding your lop rabbit fresh fruits and vegetables, make sure you don't go overboard with the portions and make sure to introduce new foods slowly. Always keep an eye on your rabbit's digestion to make sure he tolerates the new foods well. Consult your veterinarian if he develops any kind of digestive problems after feeding him a new food.

Tips for Feeding Lop Rabbits

Now that you know what to feed your lop rabbit you may be wondering when and how much to feed him. To make sure that your rabbit gets the nutrients he needs, you need to adjust his diet based on his age. For example, baby rabbits that have just been weaned can benefit from higher protein content in their diet while adult rabbits need more fiber than protein. <u>Below you will find an overview of the ideal composition of a lop rabbit's diet as determined by his or her age</u>:

Baby Rabbits (Birth to 7 months)

- **From birth to 3 weeks** – mother's milk only
- **From 3 to 4 weeks** – mother's milk, small portions of pellets and alfalfa hay
- **From 4 to 7 weeks** – mother's milk, free access to pellets and alfalfa hay
- **From 7 weeks to 12 weeks** - unlimited access to pellets and alfalfa hay
- **From 12 weeks to 7 months** – introduce veggies one at a time, unlimited access to pellets and alfalfa hay

Young Adult Rabbits (7 months to 12 months)

- Introduce timothy hay, grass hay, oat hay, and other hays while decreasing alfalfa hay
- Decrease pellet consumption to ½ cup per 6 pounds of bodyweight
- Increase daily consumption of vegetables to 1 cup per 6 pounds of bodyweight
- Introduce fruit in small quantities – no more than 1 to 2 ounces per 6 pounds bodyweight

Mature Adult Rabbits (1 year to 5 years)

- Unlimited daily access to timothy hay, oat hay, and other grass hays
- Decrease to ¼ to ½ cup pellets per 6 pounds bodyweight

- At least 2 cups fresh veggies per 6 pounds bodyweight daily
- Fruit ration no more than 2 ounces (about 2 tbsp.) per 6 pounds bodyweight daily

Senior Rabbits (6 years and older)

- Continue adult diet as long as healthy weight is maintained
- Offer unlimited access to pellets if needed to keep weight up
- Offer alfalfa hay to underweight rabbits as long as calcium levels are within the normal range

Dangerous Foods to Avoid

In addition to knowing what foods you should be feeding your lop rabbit, you should also be aware of some foods that are dangerous or toxic to rabbits. <u>Here is a list of foods to avoid feeding your lop rabbit</u>:

- Avocado
- Beets
- Bread
- Chocolate
- Coffee
- Citrus peels
- Corn
- Fresh peas
- Grains

- Green beans
- Legumes
- Nuts
- Onions
- Potatoes
- Rice
- Rhubarb leaves
- Seeds
- Sugar

If your rabbit eats any of these foods, contact the Pet Poison Control hotline right away at (888) 426 – 4435.

Chapter Six: Breeding Your Lop Rabbit

Nothing is more adorable than a little baby lop rabbit – except for maybe a whole litter of them! Lop rabbits are friendly and adorable which makes many rabbit owners consider breeding. What you need to realize, however, is that breeding your rabbit is not a decision that should be made lightly. Breeding rabbits is a big responsibility and you should only do it if you can do it right. In this chapter you will learn the basics about breeding rabbits and raising kits (baby rabbits) to help you decide whether or not you are truly up to the task.

Basic Rabbit Breeding Information

Before you can breed your lop rabbit, you need to understand the basics of rabbit breeding. Most rabbits are mature enough to be mated by the time they reach 4 to 4 ½ months old. Keep in mind that miniature breeds like the Mini Lop or the Dwarf Lop – as well large breeds like the English Lop – may take a little longer to mature. For the health and safety of your female rabbit, it is recommended that you wait until female rabbits of larger breeds are about 6 months old. You can always ask your veterinarian if you aren't sure about your specific lop rabbit.

When your lop rabbits are old enough for breeding, you can introduce the male and female to encourage mating.

The best practice is to take the doe (the female) to the male's cage. If you do it the other way around the buck will probably waste time marking his territory in the new cage and the doe may even become aggressive and territorial toward him. Once you introduce the female to the male's cage, it shouldn't be long before he makes a brief display of courtship behavior and then mounts the female. When the male grunts and falls backward or to the side, you know that the mating has been completed successfully.

To increase the chances of pregnancy, many lop rabbit breeders choose to mate their rabbits a second time after one hour. Other breeders prefer to breed the same pair about 24 hours later. It is up to you what kind of schedule you want to follow, but your chances of success will be higher if you allow the pair to mate more than once. If you have multiple female rabbits you want to breed, you may really only need one buck, though it couldn't hurt to have a backup. Just be careful about choosing your pairings because you don't want to engage in any inbreeding.

You won't be able to tell immediately whether your lop rabbit doe is pregnant but you should be able to palpate her abdomen and feel the kits by about 14 days after mating. Be very careful as you do this to avoid harming the kits. Hold the doe down gently with one hand and use the other to feel the belly just in front of the pelvis area. If the doe is pregnant you should be able to feel several marble-sized embryos. If the doe is not pregnant you can rebreed her and check again after 2 weeks. If the doe is pregnant, wait about two weeks before adding a nesting box to the cage.

Raising Baby Lop Rabbits

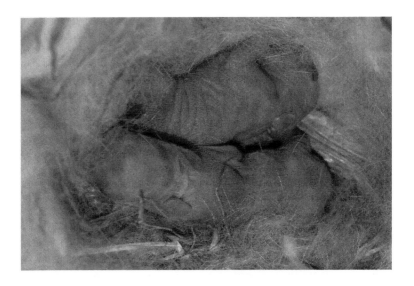

After mating, the nesting box should be provided for your doe lop rabbit at about day 28, about 3 days before you can expect her to give birth. There is no reason to place the nesting box any earlier because the rabbit will either use it as a litter box or mess around with it so much that you need to replace the bedding. The nesting box should be about 18 inches long, 10 inches wide, and 10 inches high. Cut the front with a V-shape or taper it down to about 6 inches so the do can easily climb in and out.

To prevent moisture buildup in the nesting box, keep the top open and line the bottom with ¼-inch mesh. Fill the nesting ox with soft straw, pine shavings, or hay. As long as you add the nesting box about 3 days before delivery, the doe will pull out her own hair and add it to the bedding to make a soft nest for her young. The doe should give birth somewhere between 31 and 34 days after mating. The average litter size for lop rabbits depends on the breed. Small breeds like the Dwarf Lop or Mini Cashmere Lop may only have two kits while larger breeds like the English Lop may have 10 kits. Average-sized lop rabbits can be expected to have about 6 kits per litter.

As soon as the kits are all born you need to check the litter and make sure to remove any that are still-born. Lop rabbits are very small when they are born and because they have no hair and closed eyes, they are completely dependent on their mother. Their fur will start to grow in after 5 or 6 days and they will open their eyes after about 10 to 12 days. Sometimes the kits will have crust over their eyes that prevents them from opening – just wipe them carefully with a damp cloth.

Unfortunately, the mortality rate for baby rabbits is fairly high – around 40%. To help reduce this number you should keep the nest box clean and dry. There is no need to clean the box after the first week, but do keep an eye out to make sure it doesn't get too damp or dirty. You should also be mindful about feeding your doe a healthy diet so the nutrients are passed on to her kits. Do not be surprised if the doe spends most of her time out of the nesting box – she will generally only return to feed the kits two or three times a day. After 3 weeks of this, the kits will start to leave the nesting box on their own.

Once your litter of kits has started to leave the nest box, you can think about rebreeding your doe. Does typically reduce their milk production at the 3-week mark but if you breed the doe again about 2 to 3 weeks after kindling you can extend milk production and start weaning the kits at about 4 weeks old. Just keep a close eye on the health and wellness of your doe and your kits to determine the best course of action.

Chapter Seven: Grooming Your Lop Rabbit

Different lop rabbit breeds have different coat lengths and textures so take the time to explore your rabbit's coat in order to determine what his grooming needs might be. In this chapter you will receive tips for choosing the right grooming tools for your lop rabbit and for keeping his coat in good condition. You will also receive instructions for other necessary grooming tasks such as trimming your rabbit's nails, cleaning your rabbit's ears, and keeping your rabbit's teeth healthy. Do not underestimate the importance of grooming in caring for your lop rabbit!

Recommended Tools to Have on Hand

In order to keep your rabbit's coat clean and in good condition you will need to have a few grooming tools on hand. The most important thing you are going to need is a good brush. The type of brush you need will depend on which breed of lop rabbit you have and which type of coat he has. If you have a long-haired lop rabbit like the American Fuzzy Lop you should be prepared to spend a little more time grooming his coat than you would a short-coated breed like the Mini Lop. You may even want to trim your lop rabbit's coat to keep it from getting too out of control with tangles and mats.

Here are some of the grooming tools that may come in handy when it comes to grooming your lop rabbit:

- Slicker brush (no metal teeth)
- Wire-pin brush
- Wide-toothed comb
- Small, sharp scissors
- Nail clippers
- Flea comb
- Styptic powder
- Cotton balls
- Mild antiseptic solution

Learning how to groom your rabbit effectively is a task that takes time to learn. If you have no idea where to start, it wouldn't be a bad idea to talk to a fellow rabbit owner or take your rabbit to a professional groomer so they can show you what to do.

Tips for Bathing and Grooming Lop Rabbits

Most rabbits shed every three months and many rabbits go through a light shed alternating with a heavier shed. Rabbits are clean animals that groom themselves, but they will need your help to keep shedding under control and to remove mats and tangles. Plan to brush your lop rabbit at least once a week – this is sufficient for short-coated breeds, though lop rabbits with longer coats may need to be brushed daily or at least a few times a week. You will get a feel for how often to brush your rabbit as you see how much he sheds on a regular basis.

While brushing your lob rabbit is highly recommended, bathing him is not. You may be surprised to learn that most rabbits hate getting wet and giving your rabbit a bath could actually be extremely stressful for him. The only time where a bath could be beneficial for your rabbit is if he has a high fever and your vet recommends a cooling bath to bring down his body temperature. It takes a rabbit a very long time to dry, so bathing could actually put your rabbit at risk for pneumonia. You are better off spot-cleaning his coat as needed with a damp cloth.

Other Grooming Tasks

In addition to brushing your lop rabbit on a regular basis, there are some other simple grooming tasks you should be prepared to perform fairly often. These include trimming your rabbit's nails, cleaning his ears, and taking care of his teeth.

Trimming Your Rabbit's Nails

When trimming your rabbit's nails you need to be very careful. Your rabbit's nails each contain a quick – that is the pink part at the base of the nail that contains the blood vessel and nerves for that nail. If your clip your rabbit's nails too short, you could sever the quick – not only will that be painful for your rabbit, but it could lead to profuse bleeding as well. When trimming your rabbit's nails, it is best to just trim off the sharp tip. Always keep some styptic powder handy to stop the bleeding in case you cut the nail too short.

Cleaning Your Rabbit's Ears

Because your lop rabbit's ears hang down on either side of his head, he may be more prone to ear infections that rabbits with erect ears. If your rabbit's ears get wet, they could harbor bacteria growth which could lead to an infection. Rabbits with erect ears have a lower risk for infection because their ears are open and get plenty of air flow. If you need to clean your rabbit's ears, dip a cotton ball in a mild antiseptic solution and squeeze out any excess liquid. Use the cotton ball to wipe any ear wax or debris from your rabbit's ears then let them air dry.

Caring for Your' Rabbit's Teeth

Many rabbit owners do not realize that their rabbit's teeth grow continuously. It is entirely possible for your rabbit's teeth to become overgrown which could cause him difficulty with eating. Your rabbit has four large incisors at the front of his mouth which are used to slice through vegetation – there are two upper and two lower. But there is also a pair of smaller incisors called peg teeth which are located just behind the upper incisors. Your rabbit also has eight cheek teeth further back in his mouth which are used to grind food into smaller pieces.

Because your rabbit's teeth grow continuously, you need to make sure he gets the right kind of food that will wear his teeth down, preventing overgrowth. If you feed your rabbit a pellet-only diet, you shouldn't be surprised if he develops dental problems such as malocclusion. Malocclusion is when the teeth don't meet properly. Making sure your rabbit gets plenty of dietary fiber is the key to keeping his teeth properly worn down. You should also have your rabbit's teeth checked by a veterinarian twice a year – he can trim your rabbit's teeth if necessary.

Chapter Eight: Showing Lop Rabbits

Showing your lop rabbit can be both fun and challenging. There is just something exciting about being in a room full of beautiful rabbits and their proud owners, competing against each other for the prize of "Best in Show". Showing rabbits is a great experience but it does require a bit of preparation and knowledge. In this chapter you will learn more about the specific standard for certain lop rabbit breeds and receive some tips for entering your rabbit in a show. This information will help you to decide if showing your lop rabbit is really something you want to do.

Lop Rabbit Breed Standards

Before entering your lop rabbit into a show, you need to make sure that he meets all of the qualifications. Judging for rabbit shows is based on the standard for each breed which is published by the governing body that is holding the show – generally the ARBA in the United States or the BRC in the U.K. Make sure that you have a copy of the breed standard for whatever show you plan to enter and compare your rabbit to that standard. If your rabbit doesn't meet the qualifications, you should not enter him in the show because you will be disqualified. In the following pages you'll find an overview of lop rabbit breed standards.

American Fuzzy Lop (ARBA) Summary of Breed Standard:

Total Points (100)

- **(General Type)** – 75 points
  - **Body** – 30 points
  - **Head** – 30 points
  - **Ears** – 10 points
  - **Feet & Legs** – 5 points
- **(Wool)** – 15 Points
  - **Density** – 8 points
  - **Texture** – 5 points
  - **Length** – 2 points
- **Color & Markings** – 5 points
- **Condition** – 5 points

Faults: Long narrow body, narrow shoulders. Narrow, long or angular head. Folded ears, poor ear carriage, and wool covering the ears. Unmatched toenails on broken rabbits. Excessively coarse or hair-like wool.

Disqualifications: Excessively soft and silky type wool. Wool under 1 ½ inches in length.

Mini (Cashmere) Lop (BRC) Summary of Breed Standard:

Total Points (100)

- **Type and Condition** – 30 points

- **Head, Ears and Crown** – 30 points
- **Coat** – 30 Points
- **Color** – 10 points

Faults: white hairs in solid-colored rabbits and white toenails in colored rabbits. Coats that are wooly, matted, harsh, or extremely soft.

Disqualifications: Malocclusion, deformities, abnormalities, parasites, ill health, waviness in coat, any changes or alterations to the natural appearance.

Dwarf Lop (BRC) Summary of Breed Standard:

Total Points (100)

- **Type and Condition** – 30 points
- **Head, Ears, Crown and Eyes** – 25 points
- **Coat** – 20 Points
- **Guard Hairs** – 10 points
- **Color** – 15 points

Faults: Narrow shoulders, long in body, narrow head. Ears carried back or not fully lopped. Coat too short. Excessive white hairs in colored rabbits.

Disqualifications: Weight over 5 ¼ pounds, weight under 4 ¼ pounds. Poor condition, runny eyes, putty nose.

Malocclusion. Bunches of white hairs or white toenails in colored rabbits. Odd colored or wall eyes.

English Lop Summary of Breed Standard:

BRC Summary - Total Points (100)

- **Ear Length** – 10 points
- **Ear Width** – 15 points
- **Ear Shape** – 15 points
- **Ear Substance & Carriage** – 10 points
- **Color and Markings** – 10 points
- **Type**– 10 points
- **Straight Feet & Tail** – 10 points
- **Eyes** – 10 points
- **Size** – 10 points
- **Condition** – 5 points

ARBA Summary - Total Points (100)

- **(General Type** – 85 points)
  - **Body** – 35 points
  - **Head** – 10 points
  - **Ears** – 33 points
  - **Feet & Legs** – 3 points
  - **Bone** – 4 points
- **Fur** – 5 points
- **Color and Markings** – 4 points

- **Condition** – 4 points

French Lop Summary of Breed Standard:

BRC Summary - Total Points (100)

- **Type**– 30 points
- **Head, Ears, Crown and Eyes** – 35 points
- **Coat** – 15 Points
- **Condition** – 10 points
- **Color** – 11 points

Faults: Poorly muscled, loose skin over hind legs. Body too long or too lean. Pimpled or damaged ears, poor ear carriage. Crown not developed. Bowed or splayed legs. Excessive white in colored rabbits.

Disqualifications: Adult weight under 10 points. Malocclusion. White toenails in colored rabbits, putty nose.

ARBA Summary - Total Points (100)

- **(General Type)**– 83 points
  - **Body** – 40 points
  - **Head** – 15 points
  - **Ears** – 15 points
  - **Feet & Legs** – 3 points
  - **Bone** – 10 points
- **Fur** – 8 points

- **Color & Markings** – 4 Points
- **Condition** – 15points

Faults: Long, narrow body; raciness. Pointed muzzle, flat crown. Blemishes. Poor ear carriage, folded, narrow, or very thin ears. Weak ankles. Silky coat, long, harsh, or extremely short coat.

Disqualifications: Fine bone. General toenail disqualifications apply. Complete absence of any head markings on broken pattern. Broken patterns with less than 10% coloration.

German Lop (BRC) Summary of Breed Standard:

Total Points (100)

- **Overall Type and Shape** – 30 points
- **Head and Crown** – 20 points
- **Ears** – 20 points
- **Coat** – 15 Points
- **Color or Pattern** – 10 points
- **Condition** - 5 points

Disqualifications: Adult weight over 8 ½ pounds, U/5 month weigh over 6 ½ pounds. Putty nose on butterfly pattern. White patches on colored rabbits.

Meissner Lop (BRC) Summary of Breed Standard:

Total Points (100)

- **Type** – 20 points
- **Weight** – 10 points
- **Fur** – 20 points
- **Head and Ears** – 15 points
- **Color Silvering & Evenness** – 15 points
- **Undercolor** – 15 points
- **Condition** – 5 points

Faults: Minor deviation in type. Poor ear carriage. Deviation from ideal ear length.

Disqualifications: Major faults in body shape, fur, and color. Lack of lop type. Bad development of coat. Level or slightly erect ears. Length of ears under 36cm or over 42 cm.

Miniature Lop (BRC) Summary of Breed Standard:

Total Points (100)

- **Type and Weight** – 30 points
- **Coat, Head, Crown, and Eyes** – 20 points
- **Ears** – 30 points
- **Color and Pattern** – 15 points
- **Condition** – 5 points

Faults: Body too long, head not characteristic of the breed. Pimpled or damaged ears, poor ear carriage, ears folded. Large dewlaps in does. Rear feet not parallel to body. Fur slightly soiled or matted. Long toenails.

Disqualifications: malocclusion. Over 3.8 pounds. Deformities or abnormalities. Feet bowed or bent. Incorrect eye color. Parasite infection. Soiled or matted coat, sore pads. Any evidence of preparation (trimming, dyeing, etc.)

Miniature Lion Lop (BRC) Summary of Breed Standard:

Total Points (100)

- **Weight and Type** – 25 points
- **Coat** – 20 points
- **Head, Crown, Eye Color & Ears** – 20 Points
- **Mane** – 20 points
- **Color and Pattern** – 10 points
- **Condition** – 5 points

Faults: Long coat on ears or body, excessively short or long mane. Head not characteristic of the breed. Poor ear carriage, ears folded, crown not developed. Light soiling of the feet, ears, or genital organs. Long toenails.

Disqualifications: Complete lack of mane. Malocclusions. Over the weight limit. Deformities or abnormalities. Crooked tail. Any discernible illness. Incorrect eye color.

Blindness or partial blindness. Much soiling or matting, sore pads, evidence of irregular preparation.

Holland Lop (ARBA) Summary of Breed Standard:

Total Points (100)

- **(General Type)** – 84 points
    - **Head** – 24 points
    - **Ears** – 10 points
    - **Crown** – 8 points
- **Body** – 32 points
- **Bone** – 10 Points
- **Fur** – 7 points
- **Color & Markings** – 4 points
- **Condition** – 5 points

Faults: Body lacking depth. Pinched muzzle, flat cheeks, or narrowness between eyes. Thin, narrow ear openings or folded, poorly furred ears. Lack of strongly defined crown. Severely long or fine bone. Thin, silky, harsh, soft fur.

Disqualifications: General toenail disqualifications apply. Solid pattern rabbits. Foreign colored spots. Eye color other than specified.

Preparing Your Rabbit for Show

After making sure that your lop rabbit is an excellent specimen of the breed, you can start thinking about entering a show. The first thing you need to do is become a member of whatever organization you hope to show your rabbit with – this will likely be either the ARBA or the BRC. Once you have become a member you will be able to register your rabbit under your name and enter him in shows. It can sometimes take a little while to complete this process so stay up to date with shows in your area so you can enter your rabbit as soon as your registration is completed.

When you are ready to enter your rabbit into a show, start by reading the rules and regulations for that specific show. In most cases, registering your rabbit for a show is fairly easy but you want to make sure you don't overlook anything that might get you disqualified. Make sure you adhere to the deadlines for registration and have all of the information you are likely to need handy. <u>This may include the following</u>:

- Your name and address
- The breed of your rabbit
- Your rabbit's color and age
- The sex of your rabbit
- Whether you bred or transferred the rabbit
- Whether you are a juvenile exhibitor

Once you have registered your rabbit all that is left is to wait until the show day. Prior to the day of show, make sure that you know how to get there and make sure you have a copy of the schedule so you know exactly when your rabbit is to be shown. In the days leading up to the show you should put together a kit of items that may come in handy on show day. <u>These may include</u>:

- Your registration information
- Food and water for your rabbit
- Nail clippers – for emergency nail trimming
- Hydrogen peroxide – for cleaning injuries and spots on white coats
- Slicker brush and other grooming supplies

- Business cards, contact information
- Paper towels and wet wipes
- Scrap carpet square – for last-minute grooming
- Collapsible stool – when chairs are not available
- Extra clothes, food, and water for self

On the day of the show, plan to arrive at the venue at least 30 minutes prior to judging then proceed to your assigned pen. At this point, the best thing to do is to sit back and watch – you can learn a lot just by observing at a rabbit show. When it comes time for judging, all you can really do is wait and let the judges do their duties. Your rabbit must remain in his pen for the duration of the judging. If you rabbit wins anything, a prize card will be placed on his pen. When the judging is over, you can take your prize cards to the secretary and collect your prize money.

At this time, you can feel free to leave the show or you can stick around to keep learning. Take advantage of this opportunity to connect with other rabbit owners – you never know what you might learn or how a new connection could benefit you!

Chapter Nine: Keeping Your Rabbit Healthy

Feeding your lop rabbit a high-quality diet is the best way to ensure his health and wellness. As important as nutrition is for your rabbit, however, you also need to be mindful of certain diseases and health problems. While you may not be able to prevent your rabbit from getting sick in certain situations, you can be responsible in educating yourself about the diseases that could affect your rabbit. The more you know about these potential health problems, the better you will be able to identify them and to seek immediate veterinary care when needed.

Common Health Problems Affecting Rabbits

Pet rabbits can be affected by a number of different health problems and they are generally not specific to any particular breed. Feeding your rabbit a nutritious diet will go a long way in securing his total health and wellbeing, but sometimes rabbits get sick anyway. If you want to make sure that your rabbit gets the treatment he needs as quickly as possible you need to learn how to identify the symptoms of disease. These symptoms are not always obvious, either – your rabbit may not show any outward signs of illness except for a subtle change in behavior.

The more time you spend with your rabbit, the more you will come to understand his behavior – this is the key to catching health problems early. At the first sign that something is wrong with your rabbit you should take inventory of his symptoms – both physical and behavioral – so you can relay them to your veterinarian who will then make a diagnosis and prescribe a course of treatment. The sooner you identify these symptoms, the sooner your vet can take action and the more likely your rabbit will be to make a full recovery.

Rabbits are prone to a wide variety of different diseases, though some are more common than others. For the benefit your rabbit's long-term health, take the time to learn the causes, symptoms, and treatment options for some of the most common health problems. These may include the following:

- Abscesses
- Calcivirus
- Coccidiosis
- Malocclusion
- E. Cuniculi
- Myxomatosis
- Pasteurella
- Pneumonia
- Ringworm
- Skin Mites
- Urine Burn

Keep reading to learn more about these diseases including their potential causes, symptoms and treatment options. The more you know about these things, the better you will be able to identify them.

Abscesses

An abscess is a pocket of fluid and pus generally caused by a bacterial infection. These are fairly common in domestic rabbits and they can form anywhere on the rabbit's body. The cause of an abscess could be any number of things including a bite, a cut, or some other kind of wound – they may also be caused by foreign bodies becoming embedded in the rabbit's skin or mouth. They can also be the result of wounds in the mouth caused by dental disease.

A mouth abscess can be very painful for your lop rabbit and it may cause him to stop eating – he may also drool and drop bits of food when he does eat. Abscesses on the skin usually appear as hard lumps. The best treatment for an abscess is to drain the fluid and pus – this is usually performed under general anesthesia. Following the drainage, the wound must be kept clean and the rabbit should take antibiotics to prevent infection. Painkillers may also be prescribed.

Calcivirus

Also known as viral hemorrhagic disease (VHD), rabbit calcivirus disease is a viral disease that is highly infectious, particularly among wild rabbits. This disease causes severe fever accompanied by inflammation of the intestines, damage to the lymph nodes, and even liver damage. If left untreated, calcivirus can lead to a condition affecting the blood which prevents it from coagulating – it can also lead to massive ruptures of blood vessels in various organs.

Unfortunately, most rabbits affected by calcivirus do not show any outward signs and many die within 24 hours of the onset of fever. Some of the symptoms that your rabbit may show include difficulty breathing, weight loss, lethargy, paralysis, and convulsions. This disease is spread through direct contact or through contact with contaminated food, water or bedding. There is no effective treatment for this disease and it is usually fatal.

Coccidiosis

This disease is incredibly common in rabbits all over the world and it is caused by a protozoa called *Eimeria* protozoa. There are two types of coccidiosis in rabbits – hepatic and intestinal. Hepatic coccidiosis affects the liver and it is most commonly seen in young rabbits. Intestinal coccidiosis affects the intestines and can occur in any rabbit. This disease is transmitted through contaminated feed or water and, even if a rabbit recovers, he may remain a carrier of the disease and can pass it to others.

Rabbits with hepatic coccidiosis generally exhibit reduced appetite and poor coat condition. In most cases, the rabbit does shortly after symptoms appear. Rabbits with intestinal coccidiosis usually have a mild case with few to no symptoms – certain laboratory tests may be needed to make a diagnosis. Improving sanitation in the rabbit's cage is effective in eliminating hepatic coccidiosis, though it may not be as effective for intestinal coccidiosis.

E. Cuniculi

This disease is caused by a small protozoan parasite called *Encephalitozoon Cuniculi*. This parasite can be absorbed into the rabbit's body through the intestines and it generally causes lesions on the kidneys, brain, and other organs. Researchers estimate that as many as 50% of domestic rabbits carry this parasite in their bodies but only a small percentage actually develop problems. This parasite can even be passed down from mother to baby or through direct contact with an infected rabbit.

The most common symptoms of E. Cuniculi include loss of balance, head tilt, tremors, convulsions, blindness, partial paralysis, and coma or death. The treatment most commonly prescribed for this disease is Panacur – it can be administered in a 28-day course to destroy the parasite, though some veterinarians recommend retreatment four times a year to prevent reinfection. It is important to note, however, that this treatment is only affective in killing the parasite before symptoms appear. Plus, even if your rabbit responds to treatment he may be left with a permanent disability such as head tilt.

Myxomatosis

This is a viral infection known to affect rabbits and it is caused by a virus in the Poxvirus family. This disease is generally transmitted through insects and, in many cases, it is fatal. In the U.S. this disease is most commonly seen along the Pacific coast, though there are different strains that occur in other parts of the country. This viral disease has also been introduced into Australia, Belgium, and other countries where it has become a major problem. Myxomatosis is spread through blood-sucking insects like mosquitos, ticks, and lice, though direct transmission is possible.

Clinical signs may vary depending on the strain but may include lethargy, loss of appetite, fever, swelling around the eyes, and swelling or drooping of the ears. Unfortunately, there is no effective treatment for myxomatosis and it is usually fatal. The best way to prevent this disease from occurring is to protect your rabbit against external parasites. If your rabbit does catch the disease, you need to employ careful sanitation practices to prevent spread – this virus is extremely resistant to inactivation – it takes a lot to kill the virus. Rabbits exposed to myxomatosis must be quarantined for 14 days to confirm infection.

Pasteurellosis

Also known as "sniffles", pasteurellosis is a common disease in rabbits. This disease is a respiratory infection caused by the bacteria *Pasteurella multocida* and it is highly infectious. There are several different strains of the bacteria which can affect the rabbit's eyes, ears, and various other organs. When caught early, pasteurella can be treated but, if left untreated, it can quickly become chronic or even fatal. Because this disease is so contagious and dangerous, prevention through strict sanitation and quarantine procedures is a must.

The signs of pasteurella can vary depending on the strain and the progression of the disease but generally include a watery nasal discharge, sneezing, and a loud snuffling or snoring sound. This disease can also travel to the eyes, causing conjunctivitis, and to the ears, causing head shaking, head tilt, disorientation, and a loss of balance. It is also possible for this disease to affect the rabbit's reproductive tract and it may also result in the formation of abscesses (or pus-filled sores). The most common treatment for pasteurella is a 14 to 30-day course of antibiotics and supplementary probiotics.

Pneumonia

Pneumonia is fairly common in domestic rabbits and it is generally caused by some kind of infection – bacterial or viral in most cases – which leads to inflammation in the lungs. It is also possible for environmental factors such as chemicals, smoke, or dental disease to cause inflammation which leads to pneumonia. There are four main types of pneumonia all of which exhibit similar symptoms such as anorexia, weight loss, fever, sneezing, drooling, nasal discharge, eye discharge, abscesses, and difficulty breathing.

Pneumonia can result from four different types of infections – bacterial, viral, fungal, or parasitic. The type of infection will determine the severity of the disease as well as the proper course of treatment. Rabbits suffering from fever, anorexia, weight loss, or lethargy may require fluid and electrolyte therapy. Your vet may also prescribe antiviral, antimicrobial, antifungal, or antibiotic medications depending on the type of infection causing your rabbit's pneumonia. During treatment, your rabbit's movement should be restricted.

Ringworm

Though the name might suggest otherwise, ringworm is not a disease caused by a worm or any other parasite – it is a fungal infection common in rabbits and other small mammals. There are several different types of fungus which can cause ringworm in rabbits and it can actually be transmitted to humans as well. In many cases, a rabbit is infected with the fungus by another rabbit or by another household pet who is a carrier but remains asymptomatic. Poor sanitation, stress, high humidity, overcrowding, and malnutrition can all increase your lop rabbit's risk for succumbing to this infection.

The first sign of ringworm in most cases is the development of patchy areas of hair loss that are dry and flaky. Rabbits generally develop lesions on their head, legs and feet first which can then spread to other parts of the body. Most rabbits recover from ringworm without treatment if sanitation in their cage improves. In some cases, however, treatment with anti-fungal medications may be necessary. During treatment you also need to thoroughly clean and disinfect everything in the cage to prevent reinfection.

Skin Mites

Skin mites are also sometimes called mange mites and they represent one of the most common skin problems in domestic rabbits. The most common mites to cause problems in rabbits are Cheyletiella mites which are invisible to the naked eye and can be easily spread through contaminated hay and bedding. The cause of skin mite infestations is still unknown, but it is likely that some rabbits carry the mites unknowingly and problems only develop when the rabbit is weakened by stress, illness, or injury.

Skin mites feed on keratin which leads to poor coat condition and quality. The most common sign of skin mites in rabbits is patches of dandruff appearing on the coat, usually at the base of the tail and the nape of the neck. In cases of severe infection, the patch may actually look like it is moving because it is so heavily covered in mites. Treatment for skin mites generally involves ivermectin injection as well as a thorough cleaning and disinfecting of the rabbit's habitat. Regular grooming will also help prevent reinfection by removing dead hairs that mites could eat.

Urine Burn

Also known as urine scald, urine burn occurs when urine soaks into the rabbit's fur and causes severe inflammation and hair loss. This condition is common when strict sanitation practices are not followed. If you do not clean your rabbit's cage often enough or if you fail to keep his litter box fresh, your rabbit may be forced to sit in his own urine which can lead to this painful condition. This problem can also develop from a rabbit's inability to control his bladder due to some underlying medical condition or a physical inability to assume the right stance for urination.

The most common sign of urine burn in rabbits is inflammation and redness around the private area. The best treatment for this is to apply a soothing ointment. You should also take steps to improve the sanitation in your rabbit's cage to prevent a recurrence of the problem. The key is to keep your rabbit's cage clean and dry at all times.

Error! Bookmark not defined.

Preventing Illness

In addition to learning about the different diseases to which your lop rabbit may be prone, there are some other simple things you can do to keep your rabbit healthy. For one thing, you need to keep your rabbit's cage clean. Not only will cleaning your rabbit's cage help to prevent the spread of parasites, bacteria, and other harmful pathogens but it will also help to keep your rabbit's stress level low – if you rabbit becomes stressed, it could compromise his immune system and he may be more likely to get sick if he is exposed to some kind of illness. Not only should you clean your rabbit's cage frequently, but you should also be mindful of making sure that your rabbit gets the right vaccinations and you should take steps to protect your lop rabbit against parasites. <u>You will find specific tips for these things below</u>:

Cleaning Your Rabbit's Cage

When it comes to cleaning your lop rabbit's cage, there are two main goal you want to accomplish – removing debris and disinfecting everything. Start by emptying everything out of your rabbit's cage – that includes bedding, food bowls, toys, and, of course, your rabbit. After cleaning out your rabbit's cage, disinfect it with a rabbit-friendly cleaner. Distilled white vinegar is a natural disinfectant that won't harm your rabbit or leave any residues. If you want something stronger you can mix chlorine bleach at a ratio of 1 part bleach to 5 parts water – just be sure to thoroughly rinse everything after disinfecting it.

After cleaning and disinfecting your rabbit's cage you need to do the same for his food and water equipment as well as any toys or cage accessories. Again, you can prepare a bleach solution by mixing 1 part bleach to 5 parts water and soak everything in it before rinsing well. Make sure everything is completely dry before putting it back in the cage. When you are done cleaning and disinfecting, add some fresh bedding to the cage and put everything back. As long as you keep to a regular schedule, you shouldn't have to clean your rabbit's cage more than once a week.

Vaccinations for Rabbits

Rabbits are not like dogs and cats in that they need to be vaccinated against a half dozen different diseases. There is really only one that is commonly given to rabbits – calcivirus. Your rabbit should be vaccinated for calcivirus between 10 and 12 weeks of age and then every 12 years after to maintain your rabbit's immunity.

Parasite Prevention for Rabbits

Just like your dog or cat needs to be protected against fleas and other parasites, so does your lop rabbit. Rabbit can attract the same kind of fleas that dogs attract, so consider protecting your rabbit with a topical flea control preventive – ask your veterinarian for recommendations on which brand to use and follow the dosing instructions very carefully. You should also be mindful of your rabbit's risk for mites and lice. Fur mites can cause dry, flakey patches of irritation on your rabbit's skin and ear mites can cause your rabbit's ears to become itchy and covered with wax and debris. Talk to your veterinarian if you notice any of these problems happening to your rabbit.

Rabbit Care Sheet

After reading this book you should have a thorough understanding of the different lop rabbit breeds and how to care for them. Because you have gone through so much information, however, you may need some help remembering the important details – that is where this section comes into play. Here you will find a rabbit care sheet that includes all of the most important facts about your rabbit's habitat, nutritional needs, and breeding info. When you need the answer to a quick question, this is the best place to look!

1.) Habitat Requirements

Ideal Habitat: free-run in the home with some kind of shelter or large cage with opportunities to exercise

Cage Requirements: large enough for rabbit to move freely, easy to clean, safe

Minimum Cage Size: at least 4 to 6 times the length of the rabbit when stretched out

Ideal Cage Size: at least 8 square feet of cage space with 24 square feet of exercise space for 1-2 rabbits

Exercise Requirements: at least 5 hours a day

Indoor vs. Outdoor: outdoor has more space, easier to clean, less noise and odor; indoor is safer, better for human interaction, and easier to monitor

Cage Accessories: water bottle, food bowl, hay rack, litter pan, nest box/shelter, toys

Recommended Bedding: meadow hay, timothy hay, natural fiber blanket

Bedding to Avoid: straw, shredded newspaper or cardboard, wood shavings, pine or cedar

Litter Training: place litter tray in the area your rabbit habitually uses to relieve himself

Recommended Litter: fresh hay lined with newspaper

Litter to Avoid: cat litter, clumping litter, scented litter, dusty litter

2.) Nutritional Needs

Diet Type: herbivore

Nutrition Basics: low protein, high fiber

Dietary Staples: high-quality commercial pellets, grass hay, oat hay, fresh vegetables, fresh fruits

Pellets: at least 18% fiber, purchase no more than 6 weeks' worth at a time to keep fresh

Hay: alfalfa hay is okay for babies; timothy hay and other grass hays are a staple; supplement with oat hay

Vegetables: leafy greens should make up 75% of fresh diet; feed about 1 to 2 cups per 6 pounds of bodyweight daily

Fruit: no more than 1 to 2 ounces per 6 pounds of bodyweight daily

Water: unlimited access to fresh water at all times

Baby Rabbits: mother's milk until 7 weeks; start introducing alfalfa hay and pellets at 3 to 4 weeks; unlimited hay and pellets at 7 weeks; introduce veggies at 12 weeks

Young Adults: increase timothy hay, grass hay, and oat hay; decrease alfalfa hay; decrease pellets to ½ cup per 6 pounds bodyweight; increase vegetables and fruits

Mature Adults: unlimited timothy hay, grass hay, and oat hay; ¼ to ½ cup pellets per 6 pounds bodyweight; minimum 2 cups vegetables per 6 pounds bodyweight; ration no more than 2 oz. fruit per 6 pounds bodyweight daily

Senior Rabbits: maintain adult diet as long as healthy weight is stable; add alfalfa hay or increase pellet consumption for underweight rabbits

3.) Breeding Information

Sexual Maturity (female): average 4 to 4 ½ months

Sexual Maturity (male): average 4 to 4 ½ months

Breeding Age (female): some say wait until 6 months; depends on the breed

Breeding Age (male): around 4 months

Breeding Type: multiple cycles per year, continuous

Mating Protocol: add the doe to the buck's cage; rebreed at least one for better chance of success

Palpation: should be able to feel marble-sized embryos after about 2 weeks

Litter Size: varies by breed; 2 for small breeds, 6 for average breeds, 10 for large breeds

Gestation Period: average 31 to 34 days

Nesting Box: add after 28 days; measurements 18x10x10 inches; open top, wire mesh bottom

Bedding: soft straw, haw, or pine shavings; mother will add some of her own fur

Characteristics at Birth: eyes and ears closed, little to no fur, completely dependent on mother

Fur Develops: 5 to 6 days

Eyes Open: 10 to 12 days

Begin Weaning: around 4 weeks; does will reduce milk production after 3 weeks

Rebreeding: for continuous litters, breed again 2 to 3 weeks after kindling

References

"10 Vital Pros and Cons of Rabbits as Pets." NLCATP. <http://nlcatp.org/10-vital-pros-and-cons-of-rabbits-as-pets/>

"Breed Standard." British Rabbit Council. <http://www.thebrc.org/Mono%20Breeds%20Standards%202016-2020.pdf>

"Breeding." AZ Rabbits. <http://www.azrabbits.com/useful-information/breeding.html>

"Choosing Your Pet Rabbit." House Rabbit Resource Network. <http://rabbitresource.org/care-and-health/you-and-your-rabbit/choosing-your-pet-rabbit/>

"Cleaning Rabbit Cages." Rabbit Breeders. <http://rabbitbreeders.us/cleaning-rabbit-cages>

"Different Lop Breeds." Pets on Mom.me. <http://animals.mom.me/different-lop-breeds-5514.html>

"Disorders and Diseases of Rabbits." The Merck Manual Pet Health Edition. <http://www.merckvetmanual.com/pethealth/exotic_pets/rabbits/disorders_and_diseases_of_rabbits.html>

"Dwarf and Mini Lop Rabbit." Burkes Backyard. <http://www.burkesbackyard.com.au/fact-

sheets/pets/pets-pet-care-native-animals/dwarf-lop-and-mini-lop-rabbit/#.WA41hfArIuU>

"Going to Shows." The British Rabbit Council. <http://www.thebrc.org/going-to-shows.htm>

"Housing." House Rabbit Society. <http://rabbit.org/faq-housing/>

"Housing and Companionship for Your Rabbits." Blue Cross for Pets. <https://www.bluecross.org.uk/pet-advice/housing-and-companionship-your-rabbits>

"How to Look After a Lop Eared Rabbit." Pets4Homes. <http://www.pets4homes.co.uk/pet-advice/how-to-look-after-a-lop-eared-rabbit.html>

Kanfer, Sari. "Rabbits Need Dental Care Too." Zooh Corner. <http://www.mybunny.org/info/dental-care/>

"Licensing and Registration Under the Animal Welfare Act." APHIS. <https://www.aphis.usda.gov/animal_welfare/downloads/aw/awlicreg.pdf>

"Litter Training." House Rabbit Society. <http://rabbit.org/faq-litter-training-2/>

"Lop Eared Rabbits." Raising Rabbits. <http://www.raising-rabbits.com/lop-eared-rabbits.html>

"Rabbit Bedding." Just Rabbits. <http://www.justrabbits.com/rabbit-bedding.html#gs.sqfNHnk>

"Rabbit Care." Essendon Veterinary Clinic.
   <http://essendonvet.com.au/pet-library/rabbit-care>

"Rabbit Food." House Rabbit Society. <http://rabbit.org/faq-diet/>

"Rabbit Nutrition." Vet Secure.
   <https://www.vetsecure.com/animalmedcen.com/articles/298>

"Rabbit Terms – Terminology Words Used in Rabbitry." Just
   Rabbits. <http://www.justrabbits.com/rabbit-terms.html#gs.4ub31Po>

"Rabbit Terms Glossary." The Nature Trail.
   <http://www.thenaturetrail.com/showing-rabbits/terms-glossary/>

"Suggested Vegetables and Fruits for a Rabbit Diet." House
   Rabbit Society. <http://rabbit.org/suggested-vegetables-and-fruits-for-a-rabbit-diet/>

"What Distinguishes the Different Types and Breeds of
   Rabbits?" Pet Care Tips. <http://petcaretips.net/types-of-rabbits.html>

Index

A

abnormalities 86, 91
Abscesses 98, 99
accessories 30, 32, 40, 48, 49, 52, 109
active 44, 46
adopt 40
age 5, 12, 26, 31, 63, 94, 110
agouti...15, 16, 17, 18, 20
alfalfa.. 55, 64, 65, 114, 115
altered 26
American Fuzzy Lop 10, 11, 14, 76, 85
American Rabbit Breeders Association..3
angora...3
animal movement license 25
Animal Welfare Act...25, 119
antibiotics...99, 103
antiseptic..32, 77, 81
APHIS 24, 119
appearance...3, 86
ARBA..............................3, 8, 10, 12, 14, 16, 17, 18, 20, 43, 84, 85, 87, 88, 92, 93

B

baby..5, 7, 38, 39, 43, 44, 45, 46, 47, 63, 68, 73, 101
back 6, 12, 18, 19, 21, 57, 82, 86, 95, 109
bacteria.. 31, 50, 53, 81, 103, 108
bathing 78
bed..30
bedding............................33, 34, 35, 49, 52, 53, 72, 73, 100, 106, 109, 119
behavior 70, 97
belly 5, 21, 22, 70
birth 5, 6, 63, 72, 73
birthing 5
bladder 107
bleach 109

blood..6, 80, 100, 102

body......4, 6, 12, 14, 15, 16, 17, 18, 21, 22, 46, 57, 79, 84, 85, 86, 89, 90, 91, 99, 101, 105

bodyweight 34, 60, 61, 64, 65, 114

bowls 30, 31

box..5, 6, 32, 37, 46, 50, 52, 71, 72, 73, 74, 106, 112

BRC 4, 8, 10, 11, 14, 15, 16, 17, 18, 19, 20, 43, 84, 85, 86, 87, 88, 89, 90, 91, 93

breathing 100, 104

breed3, 1, 2, 8, 14, 15, 16, 17, 18, 20, 21, 24, 30, 32, 34, 36, 39, 42, 43, 69, 70, 73, 74, 76,
    84, 91, 93, 94, 97, 116, 117, 131

breed standard..84

breeder..38, 42, 43, 44, 45

breeding 5, 30, 39, 43, 44, 68, 69, 111, 118

breeds....3, 4, 8, 9, 10, 11, 12, 14, 16, 17, 18, 20, 23, 26, 27, 28, 30, 36, 39, 41, 50, 69, 73,
    75, 78, 83, 111, 116, 118

British Rabbit Council...4, 8, 118, 119

broken 4, 15, 16, 17, 18, 19, 21, 85, 89

brush...32, 76, 77, 78, 94

buck 70, 116

budget 31, 32, 35

C

cage ...26, 30, 31, 32, 34, 40, 46, 48, 49, 50, 51, 52, 53, 54, 57, 70, 71, 101, 105, 106, 107,
    108, 109, 112, 116

Calcivirus 98, 99

Californian 12

care...1, 23, 29, 37, 48, 80, 96, 111, 118, 119, 120

care sheet...111

Cashmere Lop 11, 15, 73

cat litter 53

categories..15, 16, 18, 29

cats 28, 31, 37, 110

causes...98, 99, 101, 106

characteristics 3

cheeks...15, 16, 17, 18, 92

chest 16, 17, 18, 56, 57

children..37

chin 4

cleaning 94

clipping 30

coat 3, 4, 5, 6, 7, 9, 14, 16, 17, 18, 22, 75, 76, 79, 86, 89, 90, 91, 100, 106

Coccidiosis 98, 100

collar 32

coloring 3

comb 77

compact 14, 18

condition 6, 44, 75, 76, 86, 100, 106

conjunctivitis 103

convulsions 100, 101

costs 23, 29, 30, 32, 33, 35

courtship 70

D

dangerous 27, 51, 66, 103

defecate 54

deformities 86

diagnosis 97, 101

diarrhea 45

diet 29, 34, 37, 51, 58, 59, 60, 61, 63, 65, 73, 82, 96, 97, 114, 115, 120

digestion 59, 61

discharge 46, 103, 104

diseases 51, 96, 97, 98, 108, 110, 118

disinfect 105, 109

disorientation 103

docile 27, 37

doe 5, 70, 72, 73, 74, 116

dogs 27, 31, 37, 110

Dwarf Lop 11, 15, 18, 28, 69, 73, 86

E

E. Cuniculi 98, 101

ears 3, 1, 3, 9, 10, 15, 16, 17, 18, 19, 21, 22, 46, 75, 80, 81, 85, 88, 89, 90, 91, 92, 102, 103, 110, 116, 131

embryos 71, 116

English Lop 11, 16, 28, 69, 73, 87

exercise 48, 50, 112

export 25

eyes 46

F

facts 1, 131
feeding..58, 61, 66, 73
female..4, 26, 69, 70, 116
fever 79, 99, 100, 102, 104
fiber 25, 53, 59, 60, 63, 82, 112, 114
fluid...99, 104
food 4, 6, 7, 30, 31, 33, 34, 35, 52, 58, 62, 82, 95, 99, 100, 109, 112
French Lop...11, 16, 88
fruit..61, 64, 115
fur 3, 4, 6, 7, 11, 12, 15, 16, 18, 73, 90, 92, 106, 116

G

genes 6
German Lop...11, 17, 89
grooming 4, 30, 32, 35, 37, 75, 76, 77, 80, 94, 95, 106
grooming tools 75, 76, 77
guard hairs 3, 4, 6, 7, 17, 18, 22

H

habitat 48, 49, 106, 111
hair...3, 6, 20, 73, 85, 105, 106
handling...48
hay 34, 37, 52, 53, 55, 59, 60, 64, 65, 72, 106, 112, 114, 115
head..........................1, 3, 9, 10, 12, 15, 18, 21, 22, 81, 85, 86, 89, 91, 101, 103, 105
head tilt 101, 103
health 34, 43, 44
health problems...96, 97, 98
healthy....................1, 29, 34, 38, 42, 44, 45, 46, 48, 58, 60, 65, 73, 75, 108, 115
hepatic coccidiosis 100
history..42
Holland Lop 11, 17, 92
hutch...30, 31

I

illness 46, 91, 97, 106, 108
import 25
inbreeding 70
incisors 81
infection 81, 91, 99, 102, 103, 104, 105, 106
infectious 99, 103
inflammation 46, 99, 104, 106, 107
information 42, 43
initial costs 29, 30
intact 4
intestinal coccidiosis 101

J

judging 95

K

kindling 5, 74, 117
kits 5, 6, 68, 70, 73, 74
kittens 116

L

leafy greens 60, 114
legs 4, 6, 7, 15, 21, 88, 105
lesions 101, 105
lethargic 46
lethargy 100, 102, 104
lice 102, 110
license 24, 25, 43
litter 4, 32, 33, 34, 35, 37, 40, 46, 48, 49, 50, 52, 53, 54, 68, 72, 73, 74, 106, 112, 113, 119
loin 6

M

male 4, 6, 26, 69, 116

malnutrition 105

malocclusion 82, 91

mane 18, 91

marking...3, 70

materials...31, 50

mating 69, 70, 72, 73

mats...76, 78

maturity..14, 15, 16, 17, 18

meadow hay..53

meat 5, 12, 25

medications...104, 105

Meissner Lop...11, 17, 90

microchipping 30

milk 6, 63, 64, 74, 114, 117

Mini Rex..12

Miniature Lion Lop..11, 91

Miniature Lop 11, 90

mites 105, 106, 110

monthly costs...29

mosquitos...102

Myxomatosis 98, 102

N

nails...6, 75, 80

neck 12, 19, 106

nervous...27

nest...5, 6, 52, 73, 74, 112

nesting box...72, 73

neuter...30

neutered...32

New Zealand 12

noise 7, 51, 112

nutrients..58, 60, 63, 73

nutrition 4, 96

nutritional needs...58, 59, 111

O

offspring 4, 6
organization 3, 93
outdoor... 51, 112

P

pair.. 26, 70, 82
palpate... 70
parasites 51, 86, 102, 108, 110
Pasteurella.. 98, 103
pattern.. 6, 17, 19, 20, 21, 22, 89, 92
pellets 34, 37, 59, 60, 64, 65, 114
permit.. 24, 25
pet.. 33, 46
Pet Poison Control 67
pet store 39, 42
pets... 3, 2, 12, 23, 24, 25, 28, 48, 56, 118, 119, 131
play 46
pneumonia 79, 104
Pneumonia 98, 104
pointed white... 15, 17, 18, 22
Poxvirus 102
pregnancy... 70
pregnant... 5, 6, 70
prize 83, 95
probiotics 103
problems 47
pros and cons 36
protein.. 60, 63, 114
protozoa 100
purchase 29, 30, 32, 43, 45, 60, 114
pus 99, 103

Q

qualifications... 84

qualities 2, 131

quarantine 103

quick 80, 111

R

rabies 25

recovery 97

registration 43

regulations 24, 25, 93

reproductive 103

requirements..23, 48, 49

respiratory...103

Rex 11, 12

Ringworm 98, 104

S

sanitation 101, 102, 103, 105, 106, 107

scent 4

schedule 70, 94, 110

scissors 77

self 15, 16, 17, 18, 21, 95

selling...4, 25

shaded 15, 16, 17, 18, 21

shedding...6, 78

shoulders...3, 12, 15, 16, 85, 86

show 12, 17, 21, 30, 77, 83, 84, 93, 94, 95, 97, 100

signs 46

size 9, 12, 26, 31, 34, 50, 73

skin.. 3, 88, 99, 105, 106, 110

Skin Mites 98, 105

sneezing...103, 104

social...26

solid 7, 17, 22, 86

spay...30

spayed 24, 32, 40

standard 83, 84

stress 105, 106, 108

styptic powder 81
supplies.. 30, 32
surgery... 30
swollen 47
symptoms 97, 98, 100, 101, 104

T

tail 12, 19, 21, 22, 91, 106
taming 48
tangles 76, 78
teeth 6, 31, 60, 75, 77, 80, 81, 82
temperament... 27
temperature.. 79
tests 101
texture 6
ticked 16, 17, 18, 21, 22
ticks... 102
time 3, 1, 2, 5, 23, 37, 46, 52, 56, 60, 64, 69, 70, 73, 75, 76, 77, 79, 95, 97, 114, 131
timothy hay 53, 60, 112, 114
topcoat 15
topline 16
toxic 66
toys 30, 35
train 32, 54
treatment 97, 98, 99, 100, 101, 102, 103, 104, 105, 107
type............................... 1, 3, 9, 11, 12, 18, 34, 48, 52, 53, 54, 60, 61, 76, 85, 90, 104, 131

U

unaltered... 4
undercoat.. 3, 4, 5, 6, 15
urinate 54
urine burn... 53, 106, 107

V

vaccinations.. 30, 44 vegetables 34, 59, 60, 61, 64, 114, 115, 120

vet 34, 35

veterinarian 34

veterinary 33

viral 99, 102, 104

W

walk 47

water 30, 31, 52, 59, 94, 95, 100, 109, 112, 114

water bottle 31, 52, 112

weaning 74

weight 15, 18, 65, 86, 88, 89, 91, 100, 104, 115

white band 15

wool 12, 85

wound 99

Feeding Baby
Cynthia Cherry
978-1941070000

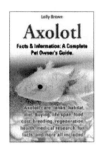

Axolotl
Lolly Brown
978-0989658430

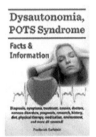

Dysautonomia, POTS
Syndrome
Frederick Earlstein
978-0989658485

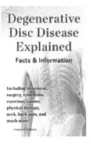

Degenerative Disc
Disease Explained
Frederick Earlstein
978-0989658485

Sinusitis, Hay Fever,
Allergic Rhinitis Explained
Frederick Earlstein
978-1941070024

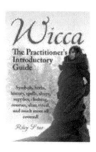

Wicca
Riley Star
978-1941070130

Zombie Apocalypse
Rex Cutty
978-1941070154

Capybara
Lolly Brown
978-1941070062

Eels As Pets
Lolly Brown
978-1941070167

Scabies and Lice Explained
Frederick Earlstein
978-1941070017

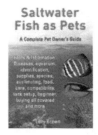

Saltwater Fish As Pets
Lolly Brown
978-0989658461

Torticollis Explained
Frederick Earlstein
978-1941070055

Kennel Cough
Lolly Brown
978-0989658409

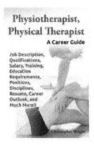

Physiotherapist, Physical
Therapist
Christopher Wright
978-0989658492

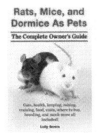

Rats, Mice, and Dormice
As Pets
Lolly Brown
978-1941070079

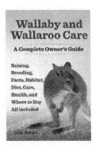

Wallaby and Wallaroo Care
Lolly Brown
978-1941070031

Bodybuilding Supplements
Explained
Jon Shelton
978-1941070239

Demonology
Riley Star
978-19401070314

Pigeon Racing
Lolly Brown
978-1941070307

Dwarf Hamster
Lolly Brown
978-1941070390

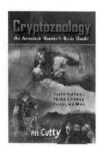

Cryptozoology
Rex Cutty
978-1941070406

Eye Strain
Frederick Earlstein
978-1941070369

Inez The Miniature Elephant
Asher Ray
978-1941070353

Vampire Apocalypse
Rex Cutty
978-1941070321

Made in United States
Orlando, FL
02 July 2023

34695651R00078